Remembering Inez

REMEMBERING

Inez

The Last Campaign of Inez Milholland, Suffrage Martyr

Selections from The Suffragist, 1916

Edited with an Introduction by
Robert P. J. Cooney, Jr.

WITH PHOTOGRAPHS FROM THE LIBRARY OF CONGRESS

AMERICAN GRAPHIC PRESS

First Edition
© 2015 by Robert P. J. Cooney, Jr.

ISBN 978-0-9770095-2-7
Library of Congress Control Number: 2014938050

Published and distributed by
American Graphic Press
P. O. Box 362, Half Moon Bay, CA 94019

agp@ebold.com
Visit www.RememberingInez.com
www.AmericanGraphicPress.com

Also available from the National Women's History Project
www.nwhp.org

Design by Robert Cooney Graphic Design
Composition and production by Marianne Wyllie

Cover and all photographs courtesy of the Library of Congress except
pages 61 & 66 (bottom), courtesy of The Sewall-Belmont House and Museum,
Home of the Historic National Woman's Party, and pages 32 (bottom) & 54,
courtesy of the Woman Suffrage Media Project.

Poems from CORNHUSKERS by Carl Sandburg. Copyright © 1946 by
Carl Sandburg. Reprinted by permission of Houghton Mifflin Harcourt
Publishing Company. All rights reserved.

Note: Both Inez's maiden and married names are used here since
she became well known before adopting her husband's name,
and then was later recognized under his name as well.

*Dedicated to
the women who gave their all
in the struggle for freedom
and equality*

The Suffragist

The Suffragist was the weekly publication of the National Woman's Party, which was dedicated to winning the right to vote for women through the 19th Amendment to the U.S. Constitution. Lucy Burns was the editor in 1916 with Joy Young and, later, Vivian Pierce as assistant editors. Burns had worked with Alice Paul, the Party's leader, since late 1912 when they took over and reinvigorated the Congressional Committee of the National American Woman Suffrage Association. Their first major effort to promote the federal suffrage amendment was a great parade in Washington D.C. on March 3, 1913, which featured Inez Milholland as a lead herald. In the months following the parade, Paul and Burns founded the Congressional Union for Woman Suffrage (which later became the National Woman's Party) and began publishing The Suffragist. Often featuring the artwork of Nina Allender (above), it covered Party activities and included the articles reproduced here on the western campaign and events following the 1916 election.

CONTENTS

INEZ MILHOLLAND TIMELINE

1886   Born in Brooklyn, New York, on August 6
1909   Graduated from Vassar
1911   Led woman suffrage parade in New York City on May 6
1912   Received law degree from New York University
1913   Led suffrage parade in Washington D.C. on March 3
1913   Married Eugen Boissevain on July 15
1916   Collapsed on stage in Los Angeles on October 23
1916   Died in Los Angeles on November 25
1916   Memorial service in the Capitol on December 25

LATER WOMAN SUFFRAGE TIMELINE

1890   National American Woman Suffrage Association organized
       Wyoming becomes the first state with woman suffrage
1893   Utah and Colorado become equal suffrage states
1896   Idaho approves woman suffrage
1910   Washington approves woman suffrage
1911   California approves woman suffrage
1912   Arizona, Oregon and Kansas approve woman suffrage
1913   Congressional Union for Woman Suffrage organized
1914   Montana and Nevada approve woman suffrage
1916   National Woman's Party organized
1917   Suffragists begin to picket the White House on January 10
       New York approves woman suffrage
1918   Oklahoma, Michigan, South Dakota approve woman suffrage
1919   Congress passes the 19th Amendment
1920   36 states ratify the 19th Amendment

Inez Milholland before the May 6, 1911 woman suffrage parade in New York City.

INTRODUCTION

Robert P. J. Cooney, Jr.

INEZ MILHOLLAND was a fascinating young New York suffragist who became a leading figure in the struggle for women's rights in the early 20th century. Her brief, eventful life offers us a window on this grand and nearly forgotten period in American history. As a fighter and beacon for equality, she personifies the historic drive for women's rights, and as a well-educated working professional, she exemplifies the deliberate choices and sacrifices suffragists made to win wider freedom for all.

A popular attorney and social activist, Inez undertook a grueling speaking tour through the western states in the fall of 1916 during a highly controversial campaign for the 19th Amendment. In late October, sick and exhausted, she collapsed while speaking on a stage in Los Angeles and died a month later of pernicious anemia, an undiagnosed autoimmune deficiency. She had just turned 30.

Her tragic and untimely death while trying to win Votes for Women aroused her comrades to begin picketing the White House in January 1917 with her words emblazoned on their banners: "Mr. President, How Long Must Women Wait for Liberty?" As they recognized, Inez suffered and died pursuing political equality for all women and so became a martyr to those who held both women and the cause of justice dear.

This brief tribute, which gathers together articles, speeches, and resolutions from issues of The Suffragist, the newspaper of the

National Woman's Party, pays homage to this fallen leader and her last campaign. It also celebrates the eloquence and passion women brought to their struggle for civil rights in the early 20th century, evident not only in the historic "Appeal" Inez delivered during her final tour but also in the many tributes to her that followed.

INEZ'S LIFE was full of complexity and contradiction. She was a beautiful socialite who was an avowed Socialist. She was an ardent suffragist and pacifist who loved to flirt and believed in sexual freedom. She was a confident, widely recognized public figure who suffered from private insecurities, depression, and self-doubts. She once described herself as "selfish and self-centered," yet she ultimately exhausted herself speaking out for others.

According to The Washington Post, Inez had "flashing dark eyes, a mass of dark brown hair and a dazzling smile." A striking personality with the hint of a British accent, she fascinated newspaper reporters and photographers. Despite a pampered upbringing, she showed concern and empathy for those less fortunate from an early age, and a forceful, independent spirit. "I couldn't stop Inez any more than one could stop the lightning," her mother once observed.

What stands out about Inez — and what is particularly relevant to young people today — is that she was a privileged young woman, motivated by a keen sense of justice, who freely chose to involve herself in the unpopular reform efforts of her day. While not abandoning her privileges, she made the decision to use her gifts to improve life, especially for women, and not to be defined or limited by either convention or her social position. As she approached her thirties, she tried more consciously to find the right balance, never losing her love of travel, fashion, and romance nor her commitment to a better world. In her final letters to her husband, she longed for a child.

This book reflects only the climax of Inez's multifaceted life, but it is the final and defining period that places her at the crossroads of a great social movement and a turning point in American history. The broader details of her life are well covered in Linda J. Lumsden's fine biography, "Inez: The Life and Times of Inez Milholland."

INEZ WAS THE OLDEST daughter of Jean Torry and John Milholland, an editorial writer, former politician, and entrepreneur who developed a successful pneumatic mail tube company in New York City. Always a champion of progressive causes, John Milholland served as the first treasurer of the interracial National Association for the Advancement of Colored People in 1910 and recruited W.E.B. DuBois to edit its magazine, The Crisis. Milholland passed his zeal for social reform on to his daughter, the oldest of three children, who they called Nan. He and his wife held ambitious hopes for Inez, believing that new possibilities would open up for her once women were enfranchised. They nurtured her independence, exposed her to culture, and groomed her for success. In New York, their stylish Manhattan apartment became a popular social center with the life and trappings of the wealthy, and they enjoyed summers at a family farm, Meadowmount, in upstate New York.

Inez's early education and first exposure to the movement for women's rights took place in England. Her family lived for several years in London while she was growing up, and it was there that she met Emmeline Pankhurst and was impressed by her zeal for women's rights. In July 1910, Inez was one of the 150 speakers on forty platforms who addressed the "monster demonstration" for woman suffrage in Hyde Park.

Tall, engaging, and athletic, Inez stood out at Vassar where she played basketball, captained the field hockey team, and set the school shot put record. She volunteered as a local probation officer during this time and the experience encouraged her interest in law. Self-confident and chafing at limits, she once defied the college president's ban on campus suffrage meetings by convening one in a small cemetery just across the road.

Inez was in her early twenties when she joined the innovative campaigns for woman suffrage in New York City led by the dynamic Harriot Stanton Blatch, the daughter of suffrage pioneer Elizabeth Cady Stanton. Blatch, who was thirty years older than Inez, also admired Emmeline Pankhurst and British "suffragettes" who were waging an increasingly militant battle for their rights. Now, Blatch and a new generation of American women were searching for the most effective strategies to win the vote in the U.S.

Earning a law degree from New York University — after being denied admission by Harvard and Columbia because she was a woman — Inez became one of the era's "New Women" and an active part of the thriving Greenwich Village scene and progressive movements of her time. She walked picket lines, offered legal advice to striking shirtwaist workers, and campaigned against child labor and capital punishment. Her talents, enthusiasm, and appeal marked her as an able young woman with enormous potential.

Strategically minded suffrage leaders like Harriot Blatch and Alice Paul immediately saw that Inez's youthful, attractive image embodied qualities sorely needed by the venerable movement. Blatch placed Inez at the front of the great New York City woman suffrage parades of 1911, 1912 and 1913, and Paul recruited her as a mounted herald in the 1913 Washington D.C. parade. Photographs of Inez on horseback, confidently leading battalions of women past tens of thousands of onlookers, raised her profile nationally and helped define the movement in the early twentieth century.

Throughout these years, Inez worked with other New York suffragists giving speeches, testifying at hearings, planning strategy, raising money, and organizing meetings and demonstrations. She also investigated and worked to improve conditions in Sing Sing Prison, won a last-minute stay of execution for a condemned man, promoted mediation as part of Henry Ford's "Peace Ship," and wrote against the war as a correspondent at the Italian front. She even found time to surprise her parents by marrying a Dutch importer, Eugen Boissevain, in 1913 after a whirlwind courtship aboard an ocean liner. "Excitement," she wrote, "is the breath of life to me." By the time she turned thirty in August 1916, she had already experienced more than many women would in their entire lives.

THE UNITED STATES in 1916 was a sprawling, still growing country where women in eleven western states could vote while those in all the rest could not. It was a time when everyone seemed "for woman suffrage" but nothing ever seemed to change. Suffragists knew they faced a daunting task. To win voting rights nationally through a constitutional amendment they needed both two-thirds support in Congress and the backing of the President, neither of which they had.

Mainstream suffragists led by Carrie Chapman Catt, head of the National American Woman Suffrage Association, concentrated on lobbying politicians and winning the vote in more states to build women's political power. The newer, more militant wing of the Association, led by Alice Paul, demanded immediate action by Congress and the President. Organizing the Congressional Union in 1913, this group concentrated on the federal government and orchestrated nationwide demonstrations, sent delegations to the President, and constantly lobbied Congressmen for the 19th Amendment. While mainstream suffragists planned a parade before the 1916 Democratic convention in Chicago, the Congressional Union formed an entirely new political party of women voters, the Woman's Party, with the single goal of equal suffrage. In the fall, they launched their most controversial and, some said, politically astute action.

Before the presidential election in November 1916, the new Woman's Party sent suffrage organizers, or "envoys from the women of the east," to the eleven western states plus Illinois where women could vote for president. For the women in half of these states, it was their first presidential election. Inez was one of those envoys who asked western women to boycott President Wilson and other national Democratic candidates to pressure that "party in power" to support the 19th Amendment. The envoys took a non-partisan, "pro-woman" stand and did not promote Republican opponents.

Inez agreed with Woman's Party leader Alice Paul that pressure, particularly the use or threat of political power, was the only thing that politicians really understood. Paul's strategy of organizing women voters to vote against one party's national candidates represented a bold new approach meant to force men in power to take notice and to make the demand for woman suffrage a national issue. Her father John Milholland backed the campaign, believing the speaking tour presented a prime opportunity for Inez to gain political experience and national exposure. She left New York for Chicago on October 4, accompanied by her younger sister Vida.

AMERICANS HAVE long been inspired by stirring words from men like Patrick Henry and John F. Kennedy. Women's voices, too, have moved Americans, inspiring courageous actions and helping to shape a common vision. Inez's Appeal to the Women Voters of the West, which is included in this book, is a classic example—a vivid work of political persuasion that captures a unique moment in our history. Addressing newly enfranchised women, she laid out a daring and controversial strategy based on their new political power, and then made the case for decisive individual action.

> "Now, for the first time in our history, women have the power
> to enforce their demands, and the weapon with which to fight
> for woman's liberation."

Articulate and commanding, Inez delivered her Appeal, in one form or another, day after day during the exhausting, all-out campaign that called for 50 meetings in 30 days in eleven states. She challenged women voters to reject party loyalty in favor of taking a bold stand for women nationwide. Her Appeal represented an unprecedented call for gender solidarity—for unified political action in support of women's rights. "It is women for women now," she declared, "and shall be till the fight is won."

She addressed herself to women—an innovation in political speeches in itself—and forcefully emphasized the importance of presenting a united front behind women's interests. In this election, she argued, women voters should exert their newly won political power even if that meant opposing male politicians who had been their allies. She told women it was time to seize the initiative and act together for the purpose of improving the lot of all women.

According to reports from the time, Inez's appearances roused great crowds and won wide coverage during stops in Wyoming, Idaho, Oregon, Washington, Montana, Utah and Nevada before she and her sister reached California. At the same time, however, her energy was being drained by severe tonsillitis and an anemic condition possibly caused by chronic leukemia. But day after day, despite her exhausted and severely depleted state, she had doctors "fix her up" and she continued on, delaying medical care until after her tour. Her passions bolstered her energy and helped her sway audiences who, unaware of her suffering, were impressed by her charismatic personality and unwavering conviction.

In Inez's busy life, suffrage was one cause among many, but during the political campaign of 1916, she realized that "this great question of women's liberty comes first."

> "It is only for a little while. Soon the fight will be over. Victory is in sight. It depends upon how we stand in this coming election — united or divided — whether we shall win and whether we shall deserve to win."

Mainstream suffragists joined Democrats in condemning the Woman's Party strategy as a misguided, partisan approach that would certainly hurt their cause. Alice Paul, however, answered that the U.S. was a nation of parties and that women making their demands clear to the "party in power" was just what a democracy expected. Still, it took steady nerves and rare ability to persuade voters to unseat a popular incumbent just to send a message to the ruling party. In some states, the envoys endured censure and threats but still hammered home the need for women to support women and demand that Congress pass the 19th Amendment.

"Fourteen times the President has refused his help. Therefore, women of the West, let no free woman, let no woman that respects herself and womankind, lend her strength to the Democratic Party that turns away its face from justice to the women of the nation."

Inez and her colleagues knew that their short, intense drive in the west was unlikely to pose a serious threat to the Democratic Party. However, they also knew that their efforts would capture the attention of politicians of both parties in Washington D.C. and force them to realize that women now voted in growing numbers.

While there was no way of knowing the envoys' actual impact on voters, their campaign and Inez's death in November 1916 marked a turning point in the suffrage movement that led to one of its last and most dramatic chapters. Following a poignant and dramatic Memorial Service for Inez in Statuary Hall in the U.S. Capitol, suffragists began picketing the White House holding banners bearing her final plea.

The picketing, imprisonment, and mistreatment of these women, many of whom were Inez's friends and comrades, is another story, another riveting episode in the long drive for women's right to vote. It is also part of Inez's legacy, inspired by her words, her actions, and her sacrifice.

Just over a year after Inez's death, in January 1918, the climate in Washington had dramatically changed and President Wilson finally declared his support for the 19th Amendment. Despite delays by die-hard opponents in Congress, suffragists soon emerged triumphant. They had won the vote in New York and over a dozen other states plus widespread public support. They had also achieved what had seemed impossible. In one decade, American women went from being disenfranchised and essentially powerless to gaining political equality with the highest level of government support. Just before the 1920 elections, 36 states ratified the 19th Amendment and, on August 26, it was declared part of the Constitution. The "Susan B. Anthony Amendment" is still the only place in the Constitution where women are explicitly mentioned.

THE INTENT of this collection is not to idealize or sentimentalize Inez but to remember her and to honor her sacrifice a century after her passing. Details of her colorful personal life, and legends of her heroism, might easily distract from her actual public role and years of involvement. Looking back today, she clearly was an exceptional young leader who both women and men admired, listened to, and believed in, and her loss was deeply felt. Her ambitions and imperfections were no secret to those who knew her but they did not blind them to her character or exceptional qualities. Wealth, beauty, race, and gender were all significant factors in her life, but the core of her story centers on personal courage and political commitment. She believed in democracy and she represented the concerns of women who at the time had no elected leaders. She spoke out eloquently for women, defended them, challenged them, and worked to improve their condition. When the demands of her final campaign grew overwhelming and her strength drained away, she refused to give up and spent the last of her energy in the effort to win political liberty for half the nation.

Inez Milholland Boissevain became a powerful symbol for a generation of American women. Her dedication and sacrifice offered inspiration to suffragists during their harsh imprisonments, and her influence continued after suffrage was won. Ultimately, she came to symbolize the sacrifices of thousands of women on their long drive for full equality. Like many other women, Inez could have served ably as a judge, governor, or senator had she had an equal chance and lived long enough. Still, in her brief life, she became a significant and influential figure, and even after her death, she remains a powerful and lasting presence. As a woman who gave her all in the struggle for equality, Inez calls up an entire movement and reminds us of this seminal chapter in American history.

American suffragists (from left) Elizabeth Freeman, Miss Wyckoff, Inez Milholland, Mrs. Holladay, and Miss A. Wright in London, c. 1910.

Published posthumously in
The Woman Citizen, January 1917

My Conversion to Woman Suffrage

INEZ MILHOLLAND BOISSEVAIN

I BECAME A SUFFRAGIST after visiting the East End of London under the auspices of the Salvation Army for purposes of "relief" — especially for women and children.

I was struck by the fact that all that we could give was no more than relief for the immediate want, with no guarantee that the want would not recur in the future. Such philanthropic efforts seemed to me futile — like pouring, water into a tub with a hole in it, and continuing to pour, in spite of the waste without stopping up the hole.

I decided that the hole in our social fabric must be mended, but I did not see how to mend it. I realized that it was an impertinence to be giving women soup and coal, when those women were working twelve hours a day and more, sewing covers on tennis balls for, I believe, three farthings (a cent and a half) a dozen, and working sufficiently hard to be able themselves to pay for soup, coal and other necessities — if properly paid.

But I did not see what to do to get them properly paid. After a while I found out that woman's labor was cheap labor. Still I could not understand why, since it seemed to me that these women worked just as hard and just as long as did the men for the support of their children.

One day I was taken to a suffrage meeting, one of the early one-room meetings of the W.S.P.U. and the light broke. I realized that the degraded political status of woman affected her status in other departments, economic, industrial, social. I saw that only by removing her political disability could her disabilities in these other departments be removed; no subject class has ever been other than despised. I understood that the only people who could protect and advance the interests of women, who could increase their wages, promote their welfare and prevent their exploitation, were those who were most deeply concerned — the women themselves.

Therefore I became a suffragist, believing that the way to right the wrongs of civilization and to strike a blow at poverty, was by means of concerted and intelligent political action, and the making of sound laws.

[This was the opening section of a longer article.]

Inez Milholland Boissevain left New York City for Chicago with her sister Vida on October 4, 1916, to begin her month-long speaking tour of the western states. The goal of the National Woman's Party campaign was to persuade women to vote against President Woodrow Wilson and all national Democratic candidates because their party blocked progress on the woman suffrage amendment to the Constitution. Inez spoke in seven western states before appearing on Blanchard Hall stage in Los Angeles on October 23.

A billboard in Colorado (above) publicized the controversial position of the newly formed National Woman's Party. In 1916, Party leader Alice Paul (right) sent "envoys" to the eleven states in the west where women could vote, first to recruit delegates to form the party and then to organize women who held new power as voters.

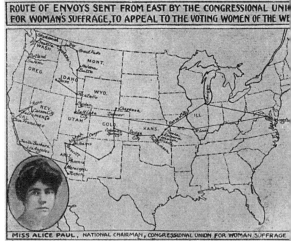

ROUTE OF ENVOYS SENT FROM EAST BY THE CONGRESSIONAL UNION FOR WOMAN'S SUFFRAGE, TO APPEAL TO THE VOTING WOMEN OF THE WEST

MISS ALICE PAUL, NATIONAL CHAIRMAN, CONGRESSIONAL UNION FOR WOMAN SUFFRAGE

The Suffragist, November 4, 1916

Eastern Appeal
Carried to Women Voters

"I WOULD ASK PRESIDENT WILSON, 'How long must we wait, how long must this heart-breaking struggle for justice go on?'" cried Inez Milholland at a great meeting in Blanchard Hall in Los Angeles. At this climax she swayed and fell. Worn out with the long campaign, the effort of speaking had been too much. The Los Angeles *Times* wrote:

"With arm upraised, condemning President Wilson for his treachery to women, before one of the largest audiences Blanchard Hall has ever held, Inez Milholland Boissevain, the beautiful suffragist, fell in a dead faint on the platform last evening.

"It was a dramatic scene. A moment before, this remarkable woman, the charms of whose personality have not been exaggerated, held the great audience with the fire and emotion of her oratory. In the middle of an intense sentence she crumpled up like a wilted white rose and lay stark upon the platform, while one of those eloquent silences befell the expectant crowd. Then the excitement broke out as doctors in the audience hastened to her assistance, and little Beulah Amidon, a dainty slip of an ardent suffragist, pleaded for calm and quiet.

"While Miss Milholland was being carried from the platform, this little lady held the audience, playing for time. Reassurances were forthcoming, and eloquent excuses made, but e'er the audience departed, Miss Milholland insisted upon returning to the platform. With pale face and torn dress, she pleaded to be heard out.

"'I come as a messenger from the disfranchised women of the nation,' she said. 'We are asking you to set us free. We have asked men in vain, nationally speaking. Never before have women had the opportunity of conferring freedom. . . . Lincoln and the Republican party freed the slaves. Alexander of Russia freed the serfs. You women voters have the opportunity to free us.'

"Then followed a damning indictment of the Democratic party and President Wilson's treachery to women. With irrefutable conciseness, she summed up the record of the present administration in its attitude to women. With biting humor she recited President Wilson's various explanations as to why he was not prepared to support the national amendment, and scathingly she showed how for every excuse he had passed tantamount legislation against his own declared principles."

The Los Angeles *Tribune* said: "It was a dramatic and forceful close to a burning indictment of American politics.

"A thousand people filled the hall. They flattened themselves against the walls and crowded the doorways to hear the famous New York suffragist but when the speaker collapsed there was no disorder. People who were near the windows opened them, those on the stage carried Miss Milholland into a dressing room and murmurs of sympathy arose on all sides."

Miss Amidon wrote: "The white figure, pale, weary, often swaying as she sat, but continuing in spite of her weakness, to give her message, was a dramatic impersonation of the price that women are forced to pay for the simple justice for which they are working. The audience was profoundly moved. At the close of her address hundreds of people surged forward to say, 'After that I cannot vote for Wilson. If suffrage means that much to anyone, I'll do my part to get it for American women.'"

The meeting proved to be the last on her schedule at which Miss Milholland could speak. At its conclusion she was taken to a hospital where she is still being cared for.

"Inez has been far from well for over a year," wrote her sister from the hospital. "She really was quite unfit to start on this tour. However, she was so keen on the idea of the Woman's Party — so keen to explain as carefully as possible to the women voters of the West how essential it was for them to stand together, that she forced herself to respond to the call and go."

MISS MILHOLLAND'S first meeting in California was at Sacramento, where a luncheon was given in her honor. At this over a hundred and twenty of the most influential Sacramento women sat down. Of this number at least a hundred were ardent Democratic women and their being present was proof of their willingness to hear the appeal of the eastern women for help and to hear the record of their own party on national woman suffrage. This audience was assembled in spite of the most energetic opposition on the part of the Democratic press, which was so afraid of what the women would hear that they even warned the women through their columns not to attend the luncheon. This only served to augment the interest.

"The San Francisco meeting was a great success," wrote Miss Doris Stevens. "We packed the ballroom to more than capacity, with a throng turned away. After the meeting a stream of women came to Miss Milholland for over an hour, each announcing she had won her vote away from Wilson. It was an inspiring meeting; very enthusiastic."

Said the San Francisco *Examiner*:

"Fifteen hundred men and women last night vigorously cheered Mrs. Inez Milholland Boissevain, militant feminist of New York, as she flayed President Wilson and the Democratic party for their refusal to confer national suffrage on women.

"The meeting was held in the ballroom of the Palace Hotel and was one of the most demonstrative political gatherings seen in San Francisco since the beginning of the Presidential campaign.

"Miss Milholland, her Diana-like figure gowned in white, was a flaming personification of the equality of women as she made her arraignment of President Wilson and the Democrats for refusing to lead the women of the nation out of what she called their political bondage.

"As many people as crowded into the ballroom were turned away for lack of seating and standing room, and it was plain from the conduct of those who heard Miss Milholland talk that she made an emphatic impression and won many Wilson enthusiasts."

The *Chronicle* wrote:

"Classical in her appearance, sweetly sympathetic, yet ringing with the militancy of her cause, this remarkable woman from out of the East, with her note of defiance and of appeal, mingled with the wit and the refinement of splendid culture, swayed the enormous audience like the winds bow the trees of the forest to suppliant response.

"Almost cynical in her exposure of the weaknesses of the Democratic national attitude toward federal suffrage, yet so clever in her repartee that those who accepted her invitation to 'heckle' were laid low by the very cleverness of her replies as the queries were sent one after another from the audience after she had concluded her speech.

"And when it was all over, hundreds upon hundreds of those men and women who had listened to this marvel of a woman, crowded forward to the platform, grasped her hands and gave testimony to their conversion to her cause, the 'Cause of Freedom for the Women of the United States.'

"It was a remarkable demonstration of the tremendous power of this woman."

A member of the party accompanying Miss Milholland on her trip wrote to national headquarters: "Good temper and friendliness were the keynote of the meeting. In spite of strong arraignments of the misdeeds of the Democratic party on the subjects of the national amendment, no one seemed to resent it and no one questioned the justice of the policy the Woman's Party had adopted. At the close of the meeting, questions poured in and after questions the people flocked around the platform, promising to vote against the Democrats. Inez Milholland was on her feet for three hours and as she was far from well the fatigue was terrific, but, as she pluckily observed: 'It was worth it. It is worth anything to make them see what we want and to start them to helping us in our battle for freedom.'"

"It is doubtful, if—even in the days of Portia—" said the San Francisco *Everywoman*, "one thousand five hundred men and women (or all who could reach the sound of her voice), of differing political faiths, sat spellbound for over a hour listening to the charm of a girl's voice and a girl's reasoning; for girl in appearance at least is Inez Milholland Boissevain. And, then, have those who came to differ and to heckle, spring to their feet and cheer to the echoes, until the ballroom of the Palace Hotel in San Francisco trembled and vibrated to the sound. This crowd had waited for an hour or more for the arrival of the speaker, and tried to hold her for another hour after the close of the meeting. And such was her triumph through all the free states."

Suffragists hung a street-wide banner across the main thoroughfare in Tuscon, Arizona (above), as part of their 1916 campaign in the west. Arizona was one of twelve states where women could now vote for president, as both the Republicans and the Democrats recognized in this cartoon (right) by suffragist Fredrikke Palmer.

The Suffragist, October 14, 1916

Appeal to the Women Voters of the West

INEZ MILHOLLAND BOISSEVAIN

The full text of the appeal which Miss Milholland, speeding envoy of the East, is spreading to the women of the golden West, is as follows:

THE UNENFRANCHISED WOMEN of the nation appeal to you for help in their fight for political freedom. We appeal to you to help us, for you alone have both the power and will.

The dominant political party—the Democratic party—has the power to liberate the women of the United States, but they have refused to exercise that power on our behalf, and on behalf of justice and of freedom. They have refused to put the party machinery back of the constitutional amendment. They have blocked the amendment at every turn. The Democratic leaders in the Senate forced it to defeat through a premature vote. In the House they have buried it in committee. Fourteen times the President has refused his help.

Therefore, women of the West, let no free woman, let no woman that respects herself and womankind, lend her strength to the Democratic party that turns away its face from justice to the women of the nation.

Politically speaking, the women of America have been a weak and helpless class without the political pressure to push their demands.

Now, women of the free states, we are no longer helpless.

Now, for the first time in our history, women have the power to enforce their demands, and the weapon with which to fight for woman's liberation. You, women of the West, who possess that power, will you use it on behalf of women? We have waited so long and so patiently and so hopelessly for help from other political sources. May we not depend upon the co-operation and good-will of women in politics? Shall we not feel that women will respond to the appeal of women, and shall we not see their hands stretched out to us in sympathy and help?

Women of the West, stand by us now. Visit your displeasure upon that political party that has ignored and held cheaply the interests of women.

Let no party, whatsoever its name, dare to slur the demands of women, as the Democratic party has done, and come to you for your endorsement at the polls. Make them feel your indignation. Let them know that women stand by women. Show them that no party may deal lightly with the needs of women, and hope to enlist your support.

Women of the western states, it is only thus that we shall win.

It is only by unity, and a common purpose, and common action, and by placing the interests of women above all other political considerations, until all women are enfranchised, that we shall deserve to win.

Liberty must be fought for. And, women of the nation, this is the time to fight. This is the time to demonstrate our sisterhood, our spirit, our blithe courage, and our will.

It is women for women now, and shall be till the fight is won.

Sisters of the West, may we count on You? Think well before you answer. Other considerations press upon you. But surely this great question of woman's liberty comes first.

How can our nation be free with half of its citizens politically enslaved?

How can the questions that come before a government for decision, be decided aright, while half the people whom these decisions affect are mute?

Women of the West, stand by us in this crisis. Give us your help and we shall win. Fight on our side and liberty is for all of us. For the first time in the world women are asked to unite with women in a common cause. Will you stand by?

Women of the West, if you can love and respect your sister women if you hate unfairness and contempt, if you cherish self-respect, you must send the Democratic party, which has abused the interests of women, down to defeat in the suffrage states in November.

Make it plain that neglect of women's interests and demands will not be tolerated. Show a united front, and, whatever the result in November, there never again will be a political party that will dare to ignore our claims.

You know that politicians act when it is expedient to act; when to act means votes, and not to act means loss of votes.

President Wilson made this plain when he supported the eight-hour day measure for railway workers. If he cared about principle per se he would himself have urged an eight-hour day. But this was not worth while. What is worth while is to act for those who have organization, unity, and political strength behind them.

We have but to exhibit organization, unity, and political strength, and victory is ours. More, I say only when we have done so, shall we deserve victory.

The gods of government help those who help themselves.

Therefore, women and sisters, and one day fellow voters, let us help ourselves.

Say to the rulers of this nation:

"You deal negligently with the interests of women at your peril. As you have sowed so shall ye reap. We, as women, refuse to uphold that party that has betrayed us. We refuse to uphold any party until all women are free. We are tired of being the political auxiliaries of men. It is the woman's fight only we are making. Together we shall stand, shoulder to shoulder for the greatest principle the world has ever known — the right of self-government."

Not until that right is won shall any other interest receive consideration. This demand of ours is more urgent than all others.

It is impossible for any problem that confronts the nation today to be decided adequately or justly while half the people are excluded from its consideration. If democracy means anything it means a right to a voice in government, and there is a reason for the conceded supremacy of that right.

Women are as deeply concerned as men in foreign policy. Whether we shall have a civil or militaristic future is of deepest moment to us. If things go wrong we pay the price — in lives, in money, in happiness.

We care about what sort of tariff we shall have. If the cost of living goes up, we, as housekeepers, are the ones to suffer.

We are deeply interested in the question of national service. We know, and must help to decide, whether our sons are to be trained to peace or war.

To decide these questions without us, questions that concern us as vitally as they concern men, is as absurd as would be an attempt to exclude the mother from influence in the home or care of her family. We say to the government:

"You shall not embark on a policy of peace or war until we are consulted.

"You shall not make appropriations for the building of ships and engines of war until we, who are taxed for such appropriations, give our consent.

"You shall not determine what sort of national defense we shall have, whether civil or military, until we co-operate with you politically.

"You shall not educate our children to citizenship or soldierdom without our wisdom and advice.

"You shall no longer make laws that burden us with taxes and high prices, or that determine how our commodities shall be prepared and by whom, or that regulate our lives, our purchasing capacities, our homes, our transportation and education of children, until we are free to act with you."

This is our demand.

This is why we place suffrage before all other national issues. This is why we will no longer tolerate government without our consent. This is why we ask women to rise in revolt against that party that has ignored the pleas of women for self-government, and every party that ignores the claims of women, until we win.

Women of the West, will you make this fight? Will you take this stand? Will you battle for your fellow women who are not yet free?

We have no one but you to depend on. Men have made it plain that they only fight for us when it is worth their while, and you must make it worth their while. You must ignore that party that has ignored women, and demonstrate to all future parties that it is dangerous to do so.

It is only for a little while. Soon the fight will be over. Victory is in sight. It depends upon how we stand in this coming election — united or divided — whether we shall win and whether we shall deserve to win.

We have no money, no elaborate organization, no one interested in our success, except anxious-hearted women all over the country who cannot come to the battle line themselves.

Here and there in farm house and factory, by the fire-side, in the hospital, and school-room, wherever women are sorrowing and working and hoping, they are praying for our success.

Only the hopes of women have we; and our own spirit and a mighty principle.

Women of these states, unite. We have only our chains to lose, and a whole nation to gain. Will you join us by voting against President Wilson and the Democratic candidates for Congress?

Inez Milholland Boissevain

The Suffragist, December 2, 1916

EDITORIAL

Inez Milholland Boissevain

THE DEATH of one of the leading figures among young American women in the suffrage movement illustrates the waste of life and power that the cruel and bigoted opposition to the political freedom of women is costing the nation.

It is a truism to say that "there is no argument against woman suffrage." There can be no argument in a democracy against democracy. But the selfish interests of political groups, fearful of the gift of freedom to a class whom they might not be able to control, keeps women battling year after year against the almost impregnable opposition of the political machine.

With the nation in sore need of women's help, this long struggle for the power to help it is arousing the deepest resentment and indignation in every independent woman throughout the country. The death of Inez Milholland Boissevain has fanned that resentment into a burning flame.

Inez Milholland Boissevain (center) with colleagues just before she began her speaking tour of the west in early October 1916.

The Suffragist, December 2, 1916

Inez Milholland

VIVIAN PIERCE

INEZ MILHOLLAND, we like to think, typified the new spirit of the suffrage movement which flowered into concrete form in the Woman's Party. All her brief life she had been a crusader, a gallant and beautiful figure, stung to instant action by injustice. She brought head, as well as heart and a thrilling spirit of combat to the causes she espoused. Liberty to Inez Milholland was not merely a word, a vague hope to generalize about, to wax rhetorical over. It was a flaming goal to be actually fought for. "Liberty" was the last word she uttered in a public speech for the Woman's Party in Los Angeles.

During the Woman's Party convention in Chicago when the idea of women standing together for women and themselves making this government a democracy in fact, was made the policy of western suffragists, Inez Milholland was one of the speakers at the great Auditorium Hotel meeting. No woman who heard her that day will fail to remember the challenge in that fiery call to women to be up and about the enfranchisement of their sisters.

In the light of the partisan labels that have been carelessly given Mrs. Boissevain since her death — no one was less partisan, no one fighting more wholeheartedly for the integrity of an ideal — those memorable words in Chicago not only call up the lovely and inspiring picture of Inez Milholland as she tossed off her hat and leaned over the table to her audience with her eyes kindling to blue flame; they epitomize the policy of the Woman's Party, the new alignment in the suffrage battle, which she believed in so earnestly and literally died for.

"Do not let anyone convince you," she said with a fervent earnestness, "that there is any more important issue in the country today than votes for women — and votes for women right away.

"There are people who honestly believe — *honestly believe!* — and they are not only Democrats — that there are more important issues before the country than suffrage, and that would be very becoming on our part to say nothing more of the matter, to retire at this time and take the crumbs from the table — if there are any. Now I do not know what you feel about such a point of view, whether it finds sympathy among you, — but it makes me mad!

"Have women no part in the world's issues? Have we no brains? Have we no heart? Have we no capacity for suffering? Have we no needs? Have we hopes? To believe that we have no part in the determining of national events is to believe that women are not human beings.

"Now there are people that do not believe that women are human beings . . . But I believe, and every woman of spirit and independence believes, that women are human beings, with a definite part to play in the shaping of human events, and that any attempt at reconstruction of this world after this war is ended is inadequate and abortive without their help. We must make the rulers of the nations feel that to attempt a reconstitution without the cooperation of women is not to be tolerated. We must say, 'Women first.'

"You men alone have not made the world so much to our liking that we can trust you with its remaking. We see under your handling much poverty, too much war, too much exhaustion, too much blasted lives, too little hope, too little joy, too few happy children. So that when the period of reconstruction arrives, together we will establish, will shape the world, or that world will not be shaped."

Inez Milholland's whole career was like a progress toward the light she saw ahead and she seemed always to move toward it in battle, but singing. In all her tilts for liberty there was nothing of littleness or rancor. As her school teachers looked upon her with a mixture of disapproval mingled with a profound but uneasy respect, so it was to the end. Men seemed to realize that she did not hate men and institutions so much as she loved liberty.

In her Vassar days, those days when young women were forbidden by the authorities to discuss the enfranchisement of women, Inez Milholland, one of the leading spirits of the college, canvassed the dormitories and found an overwhelming opinion in favor of suffrage; she proceeded to hold suffrage meetings outside the college chapel, since she was forbidden to hold them inside. While still an undergraduate, her deep feeling against social injustice found expression in work for the unfortunate children of the neighborhood as probation officer.

Her active work for the shirt waist makers' strike in New York had its root in this same desire to right industrial wrongs. When her thrilling street pleas for the strikers caused her arrest in New York, charged with "leading an unlawful assemblage," her protest at her arrest was not so much over the fact, as that the young working women who were her companions suffered the penalty of the law while her case was dismissed. From this time she was an active member of the Woman's Trade Union League, and it was her earnest desire to help industrial workers caught in the toils of the law that caused her to become an attorney.

The denial of her right to study law at Yale University on the ground of sex, aroused protest on her part that caused the feminists of the East to enter an earnest campaign which she led in the newspapers with telling effect for many weeks. Finally entering the New York University Law School, she received her degree in 1912 and opened offices in East Ninth Street, a location that would keep her in touch with those she wished to reach, men and women unable to afford to purchase justice through the services of powerful attorneys. Her first cases were successful; she could have pursued the conventional and affluent course had she not been at heart a young crusader.

Typical of this spirit was her interest in the case of Stielow, the condemned murderer whose case touched to the quick her yearning for fair play for even the most defenceless and neglected. It aroused her flaming scorn that a great state like New York should, after a cat and mouse game, in cold blood take the life of a half-witted irresponsible. Her battle on his behalf brought her face to face with the black side of capital punishment, and her recent organization of the New York anti-capital punishment campaign is still fresh in the minds of her friends.

Following her marriage to Eugen Boissevain in London in 1913, Inez Milholland found herself returning to her native land an alien. She had not considered this injustice against American women. Not for her own sake—for her husband immediately took out naturalization papers—but for the sake of other American women, crippled in their very ability to earn a living by being made aliens in their own country, she attempted to set in motion through Senator O'Gorman a Congressional enactment that would remove this disability of American women marrying foreigners.

To all of these protests for justice of the last few years of her life, Inez Milholland brought the same spirit of beautiful virile youth, glad to spend itself for an ideal of liberty. Not only the suffrage battle in this country, but many other generous movements that were touched with her crusader's spirit will remember her. Causes are made up of the gray consistent rank and file endeavor of many yearning souls. But when one of the beautiful and young and gallant dedicates herself, she becomes as outstanding as a torch in the dark. Those who came in contact with Inez Milholland will remember her as a torch that illuminated the rank and file and had the rare power of dramatizing a cause to the multitude.

WE DO NOT talk of martyrs, no, not we
Who daily watch the long and bloody toll
Taken by war and industry, and see
How common is this gallantry of soul:
We do not talk of martyrs, we who plead
To share the duties of a human lot,
Who hold the faith that Truth and Honor lead
Along a path where women falter not;
We do not talk of martyrs; yet when one
So young, so eager, and so brave departs,
Her cause unconquered, and her task undone,
A sacred bitterness is in our hearts!
How long must we be patient under wrong?
Alas, my countrymen, how long, how long!

Alice Duer Miller
The Suffragist
December 23, 1916

Inez Milholland astride Grey Dawn before leading the woman suffrage parade in Washington D.C. on March 3, 1913. She described her herald's costume as "something suggesting the free woman of the future, crowned with the star of hope, armed with the cross of mercy, circled with the blue mantle of freedom, breasted with the torch of knowledge, and carrying the trumpet which is to herald the dawn of a new day of heroic endeavor for womanhood."

The Suffragist, December 23, 1916

Inez Milholland Boissevain: "The keynote of her life was hope"

THE FINEST MEMORIAL to Inez Milholland Boissevain is to be a new consecration of her friends to the causes which she loved.

A memorial meeting is to be held in her honor on Thursday evening at Cooper Union, writes Emma Bugbee in the New York *Tribune*, but it is to be a meeting built on hope rather than on mourning. Not the pathos of the passing of one so beautiful and brave, but the inspiration which she lighted in the lives of her friends — this is to be the keynote of the meeting. It was only on these terms that her family consented to any public demonstration. They frowned on the plan to organize a big funeral, but when some one was inspired to arrange a meeting which would look to the future and put new warmth and courage into the hearts of those who are working for unselfish causes, they were glad.

"Almost her last words were 'Keep on working for democracy'," said her sister, Miss Vida Milholland, discussing the plans for the memorial meeting, "and I am sure she does not want us to mourn her now, but to hurry up and do something to make the world better. The keynote of her life was hope. She hated moping around and talking about how bad things were, as much as she loved plunging in to set them right."

So there will be a socialist, a pacifist, a labor leader, a prison reformer and a suffragist among the speakers at the meeting.

Many prominent men and women have asked for the privilege

of paying their homage to one of the best-loved figures of our day, but only those will be on the program who can seal their tributes with work in the future. In the audience will be many, too, who will never tell their stories to the public, girls whom she befriended, ex-convicts for whom she found work, and men and women to whose sordid little tragedies she gave without stint of her legal knowledge.

"The last time I saw her she was in my place trying to get a man a job."

"Whenever a woman came to me for advice, I sent her to Mrs. Boissevain, for I knew she would help her without charging her anything."

These are the stories which have come to her family in the days since she died — stories which no one ever noticed before, because the radiance of the living woman was so bright there were no eyes for the drab little figures she was holding by the hand.

Just why she chose to be a lover of democracy instead of a social celebrity is one of the mysteries which the Maker of souls alone understands. It is only possible for us to piece together the bits of her life story.

She started in as a tiny child. When sent out to play with her sister and the other "nice little girls" in Madison Square she horrified the nurse and angered the "nice little girls" by inviting the "street children" to join in their games.

"We won't play with you if you play with those Third Avenue children," the little girls said.

"You don't have to," six-year-old Inez retorted, "but I'm going to play with them. They've got just as much right in this park as you have."

It was in London, where her father's business had taken the family, that she first learned to hate poverty in the abstract.

"We missed her one afternoon, and after hunting all over we found her down at Charring Cross with a Salvation Army girl," her mother told me the other day. "That set her thinking and I date all her socialistic theories from that afternoon, although she didn't use the word 'Socialism' much until after she had been to Vassar. She got most of her radicalism there.

"She came by her interest in politics naturally, though. Because of her father's interest in the underdog our house was always full of leaders of unpopular causes. We knew John Redmond and George Bernard Shaw and such people in those days. Sometimes after I had had a dinner party Inez would say to me at breakfast, 'Who was that man that talked about Ireland so long?'

"'What do you know about it?' I would cry, and she would laugh:

"'Oh, I was out there on the stairs listening. I hid when they opened the door, because I only had on my nightgown.'

"She was very beautiful when she was growing up. More than once duchesses inquired who she was, and all my friends took it for granted that I would have her presented at court as soon as she came out. Of course, I wanted her to, but do you suppose she cared about court?

"Pooh! Why should she kiss a king's hand? She wouldn't be seen with a king, she would say, and dash off to some radical meeting.

"I don't remember just when we first became acquainted with Mrs. Pankhurst and the London suffragists, but I know I had them in my drawing room for Mrs. Pankhurst's first public meeting. It cost me two of my best friends, too, but I couldn't stop Inez any more than one could stop the lightning. She had a whole lot of members of Parliament there to meet Mrs. Pankhurst, and it was a very remarkable meeting in the light of later happenings. Inez never was arrested herself, though I held my breath in terror every time she went with them, and I don't understand to this day how she escaped, for she was absolutely fearless; but I believe we came back to America to live before the worst of the riots."

The spectacular incidents in her New York career are, of course, well known. Inez Milholland dashing up Fifth Avenue on horseback at the head of a suffrage parade and standing with stars in her hair as the symbol of America in all the pageants will be a tradition in suffrage history.

It was not her parades, or even her speeches, however, which brought half the suffrage leaders of New York, with tears streaming down their faces, to headquarters on the morning she died. . . . It was partly her sense of fair play and partly her capacity for enjoying every moment of the game.

I remember her at Vassar a year ago, when the college was celebrating its fiftieth anniversary. She was quite the most prominent of the "old guard" who came back for the ceremonies, and undergraduate attention focused itself chiefly on her.

Whenever they strolled across the campus one felt the unseen eyes of adoring freshmen peering from behind the trees, and when Mrs. Boissevain, who had made the college record for the shot put in her day, shook hands with the champion of the after years the whole college cheered. A suffrage meeting had been called by the energetic Congressional Union, of which she was a loyal follower, and to which cause she gave her life in the last campaign. The suffrage meeting did not meet with encouragement from college authorities, however, and it was called off.

"Oh, never mind! I'd much rather play basketball again," Mrs. Boissevain cried cheerfully, and hurried away to hide her beauty in a much bedraggled gym suit borrowed from a lanky sophomore. She entered into the game in that homely outfit with the same vivid enthusiasm which marked all her public doings.

Life in the same little Adirondack town where she spent her summers was the same story of happiness and affectionate interest in everyone about her, and it is there, perhaps, that the only memorial that can be seen by the eye will stand.

Not many miles away at North Elba, is the birthplace of John Brown, whose "soul goes marching on!" They are not going to sing about Inez Milholland's soul, but the people of the neighborhood are not going to forget her, for whenever they look to the mountains they will see Mount Inez, the highest peak round about there. It has been renamed by the people of Lewis in honor of their most illustrious citizen.

Amid sorrowing groups of kinsfolk, friends and neighbors, who had watched her remarkable career from childhood, the body of Inez Milholland Boissevain was laid to rest on one of the most picturesque sites of the Adirondacks. A foothill of the famous Jay Range which divides that township from Lewis, it rises gently from the little white church and graveyard west from the village and commands a view of the mountains, for its elevation, unsurpassed throughout this famous Boquet Valley.

The services were characterized by simplicity, the Elizabethtown (N.Y.) Post writes. Reverend Herbert Ford, formerly of Westminister Church, New York, now located at Elizabethtown, spoke briefly of Mrs. Boissevain's life and work, touching upon the spiritual nature that dominated more and more all her activities and the tremendous, comprehensive passionate love for her fellow creatures that was summed up in her well-known declaration of principles: "I want to make everybody happy and I want everybody to love me."

In recognition of this dominant note of her being the song service was cast: "Oh love that will not let me go," "Love divine, all love excelling," and "Abide with Me."

The pall bearers were six of the oldest farm hands employed at Meadowmount.

In all the wilderness of flowers that came from the Pacific to the Atlantic, east, west, north and south, no piece touched the heart of the family and the multitude so deeply as the large beautiful wreath of Autumn leaves filled with white chrysanthemums, from the convicts of Sing Sing Prison, for the amelioration of whose condition she labored so zealously and so successfully.

The American flag presented by the California gentlemen "to the bravest soldier and most unselfish knight since Joan of Arc" was left upon her breast with the Bible given her when a child by her mother. Her father's last token was her favorite flowers, the red rose of courage and the white lily "of a pure intent."

GALLERY

Alice Paul (in white) spoke to a New York audience in 1911 about the situation among suffragists in Great Britain. City suffrage leaders Inez Milholland and her mentor Harriot Stanton Blatch are seated behind her. Paul, who was a year and a half older than Inez, had been jailed and force-fed during the British campaign. The Woman's Journal (right) covered the March 3, 1913 parade in the Capitol which Inez (center) led and unruly crowds disrupted.

WOMAN'S JOURNAL
AND SUFFRAGE NEWS

VOL. XLIV. NO. 10   SATURDAY, MARCH 8, 1913   FIVE CENTS

PARADE STRUGGLES TO VICTORY DESPITE DISGRACEFUL SCENES

Nation Aroused by Open Insults to Women—Cause Wins Popular Sympathy—Congress Orders Investigation—Striking Object Lesson

Washington has been disgraced. Equal suffrage has scored a great victory. Thousands of indifferent women have been aroused. Influential men are incensed and the United States Senate demands an investigation of the treatment given the suffragists at the National Capital on Monday.

Ten thousand women from all over the country had planned a magnificent parade and pageant to take place in Washington on March 3. Artists, pageant leaders, designers, women of influence and renown were ready to give a wonderful and beautiful piece of suffrage work to the public that would throng the National Capital for the inauguration festivities. The suffragists were ready; the whole procession started down Pennsylvania avenue, when the police protection, that had been promised, failed them, and a disgraceful scene followed. The crowd surged into the space which had been marked off for the paraders, and the leaders of the suffrage movement were compelled to push their way through a mob of the worst element in Washington and vicinity. Women were spit upon, slapped in the face, tripped up, pelted with burning cigar stubs, and insulted by jeers and obscene language too vile to print or repeat.

The cause of all the trouble is apparent when the facts are known. The police authorities in Washington opposed every attempt to have a suffrage parade at all. Having been forbidden a place in the inaugural procession, the suffragists asked to have a procession of their own on March 3. They were finally told that they could have a procession but that it could not be on Pennsylvania avenue, but must be on a side street. At last they got permission to have the suffrage parade on the avenue, and asked that traffic be excluded from the street during the parade. For a long time this was denied, and only on Saturday were they successful.

Everything was at last arranged; it was a glorious day; ten thousand women were ready to do their part to make the parade beautiful to behold, to make it a credit to womanhood and to demonstrate the strength of the movement for their enfranchisement. The police were determined, however, and they had their way. Their attempt to afford the marchers protection and keep the space of the avenue free for the suffrage procession was the flimsiest sham. Police officers stood by with folded arms and grinned while the picked women of the land were insulted and roughly abused by an ignorant and uncouth mob.

Miss Alice Paul and other suffragists were compelled to drive their automobiles down the avenue to separate the crowds so the suffragists with the banners and floats could pass. The police officials say their force was inadequate to handle the crowds, but it is noted that there was no disorder on the avenue during the inaugural procession. It is stated that federal troops were offered to the chief of police for the suffrage procession, but that he refused their aid. At any rate, assistance was finally called from Fort Myer and mounted soldiers drove back the crowd so that a straggling line of marchers could pass through.

Not only were the suffragists bitterly disappointed in having the effect

(Continued on Page 78)

AMENDMENT WINS IN NEW JERSEY

Easy Victory in Assembly 46 to 5—Equal Suffrage Enthusiasm Runs High

The New Jersey Legislature passed the woman suffrage amendment in the Assembly last week by a vote of 46 to 5. The Senate had already voted favorably 14 to 5.

A large delegation of suffragists crowded the galleries, and when the overwhelming vote was announced there was a scene of great enthusiasm. Women stood in their seats and waved handkerchiefs and "votes for women" flags and cheered themselves hoarse.

Dr. Jekyll Becomes Mr. Hyde

Opposition was confined exclusively to the old sentimental arguments.

(Continued on Page 79)

MICHIGAN AGAIN CAMPAIGN STATE

Senate Passes Suffrage Amendment 26 to 5 and Battle Is Now On

Michigan is again a campaign State after a short lapse of four months. The amendment will go to the voters on April 7. The State-wide feeling that the women were defrauded of victory last fall will help the suffragists.

The final action of the Legislature was taken last week, when the Senate, by a vote of 26 to 5, passed the suffrage amendment, with a slight amendment to make the requirements for foreign-born women the same as those for male immigrants.

Governor Watches Debate

The debate in the Senate lasted an hour and a quarter, and was characterized by the persistent efforts of Senator Weadock and a few others to tack on crippling amendments. Several suggestions, including the disabling of women for holding office or serving on juries, were voted down in quick succession.

Gov. Ferris was among the visitors who crowded the chamber and gallery. Mrs. Clara B. Arthur, Mrs. Thomas R. Henderson and Mrs. Wilbur Brotherton, of Detroit; Mrs. Jennie Law Hardy, of Tecumseh, and other State leaders were present, supported by a large delegation of Lansing suffragists.

The final stand of the opposition was made by Senator Murtha in the hope of putting off the submission till November, 1914, and this also failed. Of the five who opposed the measure on the final rollcall, three were from Detroit.

A complete campaign of organization and education has been mapped out by the State Association. The

(Continued on Page 74)

General Rosalie Jones in Pilgrim Costume; Miss Inez Milholland on White Steed Leading the Parade; One of the Scores of Imposing Floats; One View of the Procession

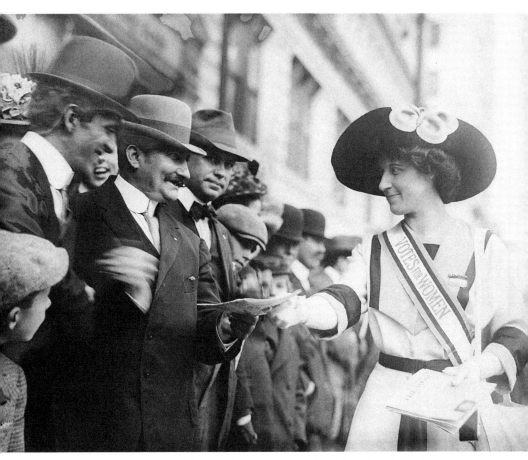

Inez was a 24-year-old law student at New York University when she was photographed selling copies of The Woman's Journal to male spectators before leading the May 6, 1911 woman suffrage parade down Fifth Avenue in New York City.

As an attorney, Inez offered legal counsel to single women, immigrants, and garment workers like these, shown during a May Day parade in New York City. During the shirtwaist strike in 1909–1910, she organized support for the strikers, raised funds, and monitored demonstrations in order to limit abuses and unlawful arrests.

New York Senator James O'Gorman (center) was the focus of a Congressional Union suffrage delegation in May 1915, led by Mrs. W. L. Colt on the left and Inez Milholland Boissevain on the right. Inez on horseback (right) prepared to lead the suffrage parade in New York City on May 3, 1913. It was the last parade that Harriot Stanton Blatch organized and that Inez led before the unsuccessful statewide election in 1915.

The National Woman's Party booth at a fair in Prescott, Arizona, brought the demand for the suffrage amendment — and for a boycott of Democratic candidates — directly to voters during the 1916 campaign. The outdoor "Headquarters" displayed copies of The Suffragist in the front and a poster advertising a Great Final Rally with Inez Milholland Boissevain on the upper left.

The National Woman's Party produced this purple, white, and gold poster to announce an August 1924 pageant in New York, "Forward into Light," which memorialized Inez and her role in the March 3, 1913 suffrage parade in Washington D.C.

Although criticized by the press and mainstream suffragists as being ill conceived and counter-productive, the Woman's Party campaign to pressure the Democratic Party echoed sentiments suffrage leader Susan B. Anthony expressed over forty years earlier. Here Mrs. James Rector, Mary Dubrow, and Alice Paul hold a banner in front of Party headquarters before the 1920 political party conventions.

The Suffragist, December 23, 1916

Resolution by the Congressional Union for Woman Suffrage

ADOPTED AT THE MEMORIAL SERVICE IN STATUARY HALL, NATIONAL CAPITOL, DECEMBER 25, 1916

WE, MEMBERS OF THE Congressional Union for Woman Suffrage, wish to express our sorrow for the loss of Inez Milholland Boissevain, a beloved and honored comrade.

This loss is measureless. Her place cannot be filled. It is not only that Inez Milholland had prophetic understanding of women; she had courage and vision and laughter. She was brave and blithe beyond most leaders—blithe and valiant and unafraid to be herself, even though she knew that self, marching in advance, with eyes on tomorrow, would not be understood by the many with eyes on today.

She lived in what women will be, in what human beings will be, but she realized that this day is without its dawn until women are free. The breadth of her vision, her dauntless courage, some vivid quality in her soul thrilled us, like being lifted into clear windswept spaces.

It is imperative that women understand her. It is not to be borne that she should pass, and that those for whom she worked should miss the luminous spectacle of her as she worked for fuller freedom. Tomorrow must not remember her better than today loves her.

She asked unceasingly that women realize themselves. Through women she dreamed humanity, a race of the self-governed, not a race half free, half bond.

These things must be divined and said: that she splendidly believed in women, that she unceasingly asked that they enter into their kingdom. She met her death preaching the solidarity of women.

Let us remember her thrilling appeal to women in her last speech:

"It is women for women now, and shall be till the fight is won.

"Don't dare to say you are free until all women are free.

"Together we shall stand, shoulder to shoulder, for the greatest principle the world has ever known — the right of self-government."

The burning figure of her standing beside all women must not be veiled from the women of the nation. She gave herself to many causes, but she put no cause before the cause of women.

Inez Milholland stood for women. She lived for women, she died for women. She is in the heart of every woman whose heartbeats for tomorrow. That tomorrow is dearer and nearer because Inez Milholland lived. We, her comrades and friends, acknowledge the great debt we owe her. In the name of all women, we accept her gift and proudly honor her triumphant death. May we have the courage and the devotion to follow where she has led.

Alice Paul secured Statuary Hall in the U.S. Capitol Building in Washington D.C. for the National Woman's Party memorial for Inez. Nearly one thousand mourners attended the Christmas Day ceremony, which filled the hall under the dome of the Capitol with music, color, and heartfelt tributes. By positioning Inez as a martyr figure, the NWP used her death as a political strategy to advance women's cause.

Mourners carrying the Woman's Party's purple, white, and gold banners followed members of the boys choir to the national Capitol for Inez Miholland's memorial on Christmas Day, 1916. Inside (right), party flags marked each seat in Statuary Hall, where no memorial had ever been held for a woman.

FORWARD
OUT OF DARKNESS
LEAVE BEHIND
THE NIGHT
FORWARD
OUT OF ERROR
FORWARD
INTO LIGHT

The Suffragist, December 30, 1916

Memorial for
Inez Milholland Boissevain

MAUD YOUNGER

DELIVERED AT THE MEMORIAL SERVICE IN
STATUARY HALL, NATIONAL CAPITOL, DECEMBER 25, 1916

W E ARE HERE TO PAY TRIBUTE to Inez Milholland Boissevain, who was our comrade. We are here in the Nation's Capitol, the seat of our democracy, to pay tribute to one who gave up her life to realize that democracy.

We are here that the life she gave should not be given in vain, but that the knowledge of her, the understanding of her, the sacrifice of her, and the inspiration of her should bring to fulfillment the work for which she laid down her life.

Inez Milholland walked down the path of life a radiant being. She went into work with a song in her heart. She went into battle, a laugh on her lips. Obstacles inspired her, discouragement urged her on. She loved work and she loved battle. She loved life and laughter and light, and above all else, she loved liberty. With a loveliness beyond most, a kindliness, a beauty of mind and soul, she typified always the best and noblest in womanhood. She was the flaming torch that went ahead to light the way, the symbol of light and freedom.

She was ever thus in the woman's movement, whether radiant, in white, pinning the fifth star to the suffrage flag when the women of Washington were enfranchised; whether leading the first suffrage parade down Fifth Avenue, valiantly bearing the banner, "Forward into light," or whether in the procession in our Capital four years ago, when, mounted on a white horse, a star on her brow, her long masses of dark hair falling over her blue cape, she typified dawning womanhood.

Symbol of the woman's struggle, it was she who carried to the west the appeal of the unenfranchised, and, carrying it, made her last appeal on earth, her last journey in life.

As she set out upon this her last journey, she seems to have had the clearer vision, the spiritual quality of one who has already set out for another world. With infinite understanding and intense faith in her mission, she was as one inspired. Her meetings were described as "revival meetings," her audiences as "wild with enthusiasm." Thousands acclaimed her, thousands were turned away unable to enter. In this western land she came into her own. Something in her spirit with its intense love of liberty found a kinship in the great sweep of plain and sagebrush desert, in the bare rocky mountains and flaming sunsets. She seemed to breathe in the freedom of the great spaces. Something in her nature was touched by the simplicity and directness of the people. And so on through the west she swept with her ringing message, a radiant vision, a modern crusader.

And she made her message very plain.

She stood for no man, no party. She stood only for Woman. And standing thus, she urged:

"It is women for women now and shall be until the fight is won!

"Together we shall stand shoulder to shoulder for the greatest principle the world has ever known, the right of self-government.

"Whatever the party that has ignored the claims of women, we as women must refuse to uphold it. We must refuse to uphold any party until all women are free.

"We have nothing but our spirit to rely on and the vitality of our faith, but spirit is invincible.

"It is only for a little while. Soon the fight will be over. Victory is in sight."

Though she did not live to see that victory it is sweet to know that she lived to see her faith in woman justified. In one of her last letters she wrote:

"Not only did we reckon accurately on women's loyalty to women but we likewise realized that our appeal touched a certain spiritual, idealistic quality in the western woman voter, a quality which is yearning to find expression in political life. . . . At the idealism of the Woman's Party her whole nature flames into enthusiasm and her response is immediate. She gladly transforms a narrow partisan loyalty into loyalty to a principle, the establishment of which carries with it no personal advantage to its advocates, but merely the satisfaction of achieving one more step toward the emancipation of mankind. . . . We are bound to win. There never has been a fight yet where interest was pitted against principle that principle did not triumph."

Into this struggle she poured her strength, her enthusiasm, her vitality, her life. She would come away from audiences and droop as a flower. The hours between meetings were hours of exhaustion, of suffering. She would ride in the trains gazing from windows listless, almost lifeless, until one spoke; then again the sweet smile, the sudden interest, the quick sympathy. The courage of her was marvelous.

The trip was fraught with hardship. Speaking day and night, she would take a train at two in the morning to arrive at eight. Then a train at midnight and arrive at five in the morning. Yet, she would not change the program; she would not leave out anything. Something seemed to urge her on to reach as many as she could; to carry her message as far as she could while there was yet time.

And so on, ever, through the west she went, through the west that drew her, the west that loved her, until she came to the end of the west. There where the sun goes down in glory in the vast Pacific, her life went out in glory in the shining cause of freedom.

And as she had lived loving liberty, working for liberty, fighting for liberty, so it was that with this word on her lips she fell. "How long must women wait for liberty?" she cried and fell, as surely as any soldier upon the field of honor, as truly as any who ever gave up his life for an ideal.

As in life she had been the symbol of the woman's cause, so in death she is the symbol of its sacrifice — the whole daily sacrifice, the pouring out of life and strength that is the toll of the prolonged women's struggle.

Inez Milholland is one around whom legends will grow up. Generations to come will point out Mount Inez and tell of the beautiful woman who sleeps her last on its slopes.

They will tell of her in the west, tell of the vision of loveliness as she flashed through on her last burning mission, flashed through to her death, a falling star in the western heavens.

But neither legend nor vision is liberty, which was her life. Liberty cannot die. No work for liberty can be lost. It lives on in the hearts of the people, in their hopes, their aspirations, their activities. It becomes part of the life of the nation. As Inez Milholland has given to the world, she lives on forever.

We are here today to pay tribute to Inez Milholland Boissevain, who was our comrade. Let our tribute be not words which pass; nor song which dies, nor flower which fades. Let it be this:

That we finish the task she could not finish;

That with new strength we take up the struggle in which fighting beside us she fell;

That with new faith we here consecrate ourselves to the cause of Woman's Freedom, until that cause is won;

That with new devotion we go forth, inspired by her sacrifice, to the end that that sacrifice be not in vain but that dying she shall bring to pass that which living she could not achieve, full freedom for women, full democracy for the nation.

Let this be our tribute imperishable to Inez Milholland Boissevain.

Alice Paul and mourners at Inez's grave in Lewis, New York.

RESOLUTION

To the President and Congress

ADOPTED AT THE MEMORIAL SERVICE IN
STATUARY HALL, NATIONAL CAPITOL, DECEMBER 25, 1916

BEYOND THE INSPIRATION to be found in the life and death of Inez Milholland Boissevain and in her last message, "Keep on fighting for democracy," there is another significance.

Those who are working in the cause for which she died, who know the thousands of other women throughout the world bearing unflinchingly its sacrifices and labors and exhaustion, turn to the President of this democracy with the plea that he intercede to stop such waste of human life and effort. For by her death there has been made clear the constant, unnoticed tragedy of this prolonged effort for freedom that is acknowledged just, but is still denied.

Because of her labor to win for herself and for other women freedom and power to play their part and carry on their life work, Inez Milholland died, and so there was destroyed what the world can so little spare, the beauty, joyousness and far-seeing helpfulness that were her gifts to it.

In all lands the strength of other women is being sacrificed, the powers of other women are being silenced, they are giving their lives to wrest from unwilling governments what is theirs in justice and in reward of service, what here and there freedom-loving peoples have granted them as a gift.

There is no need here in the United States to prolong this struggle of women. Their triumph is foreseen and welcomed. They are now fighting but the spirit of hesitancy and delay.

President Wilson, chosen chief of this republic, Representatives of the people at each end of this great corridor, we ask that you open the great doors before which our women are exhausting their lives in waiting and appeal. Will you not let this nation, by its example, win yet another victory for liberty throughout the world?

Will you not be moved to act so that by her death Inez Milholland Boissevain shall have delivered from the sacrifice of her life her countrywomen?

Three hundred members of the National Woman's Party met with President Woodrow Wilson on January 9, 1917, and presented him with this Resolution seeking his support for the suffrage amendment. However, he remained unmoved and told the women, "It is so impossible for me . . . to do anything other than I am doing as party leader, that I think nothing more is necessary to be said." His response left the women disappointed, frustrated, and indignant.

"Silent Sentinels" began picketing outside the White House gates on January 10, 1917, the day after suffragists met with President Wilson. The picketing and other demonstrations continued until Congress passed the 19th Amendment in 1919. Right: Alice Turnbull Hopkins stands before the White House with a banner bearing Inez's final plea.

The Suffragist, January 17, 1917

After Meeting
with President Wilson

A DEAD SILENCE followed the last words of the President. It was not an expectant silence. There was something stricken in it. The bitter disappointment of those hundreds of women was as keenly felt as if it had been shouted. The President paused the fraction of a second, as if waiting for applause or a stir of approval that failed to come. For that brief moment he had the subtly baffled air of a disappointed actor who has failed to "get across," as he would put it. Then the President turned abruptly on his heel and left the room. The women filed quietly from the place.

Mrs. William Kent, wife of Representative Kent of California, had invited the deputation to tea in the Congressional Union headquarters, and without breaking up the whole deputation filed back to Cameron House. There was a strange unanimity about their attitude. It was not until the deputation was seated in the great drawing rooms that the bitterness of the disappointment of these women from many states, and representing many political faiths, began to express itself.

Mrs. Harriot Stanton Blatch voiced the feeling of the body as a whole when she demanded action on the part of women in these stirring words: "We have got to take a new departure. It rests with women to go on with this fight. We have got to bring to the President individually, day by day, week in and week out, the fact that great numbers of women want to be free!"

In a ringing call for more drastic action, action that would focus the attention of the nation on the unfavorable attitude of the President, Mrs. Blatch outlined the latest plan of the Congressional Union: to picket the White House every day demanding action of the chief executive.

"We have gone to Congress, we have gone to the President during the past four years," said Mrs. Blatch, "with great deputations, with small deputations. We have shown the interest all over the country in self-government for women — something that the President as a great Democrat ought to understand and respond to instantly. Yet he tells us today that we must win his party. He said it was strange that we did not see before election that his party was more favorable to us than the Republican party. How did it show its favor? How did he show his favor today to us?

He says we have got to convert his party. Why? Never before did the Democratic party lie more in the hands of one man that it lies today in the hands of President Wilson. Never did the Democratic party have a greater leader, and never was it more susceptible to the wish of that leader than is the Democratic party of today to President Wilson. He controls his party, and I don't think he is too modest to know it. He can mold it as he wishes and he has molded it. He molded it quickly before election in the matter of the eight-hour law. Was that in his party platform? He had to crush and force his party to pass that measure. Yet he is not willing to lay a finger's weight on his party today for half the people in the United States.

"We have approached him with delegations. We have approached him with great processions. Women with full and beating hearts have individually gone to him — Republican women, Progressive women, Democratic women, to plead with him to do this thing; to do it in the name of Justice and righteousness; to do it as a great Democrat. Yet today he tells us that we must wait more — and more.

"We can't organize bigger and more influential deputations. We can't organize bigger processions. We can't, women, do anything more in that line. We have got to take a new departure. We have got to keep the question before him all the time. We have got to begin and begin immediately.

"Women, it rests with us. We have got to bring to the President, individually, day by day, week in and week out, the idea that great numbers of women want to be free, will be free, and want to know what he is going to do about it.

"Won't you come and join us in standing day after day at the gates of the White House with banners asking, 'What will you do, Mr. President, for one half of the people of this nation?' Stand there as sentinels — sentinels of liberty, sentinels of self-government — silent sentinels. Let us stand beside the gateway where he must pass us in and out, so that he can never fail to realize that there is a tremendous earnestness and insistence back of this measure. Will you not allow your allegiance today to this ideal of liberty? Will you not be a silent sentinel of liberty and self-government?"

Women picketing the White House were repeatedly attacked (above) after the U.S. entered the First World War in April 1917. In June, police began arresting the suffragists, many of whom went on hunger strikes in prison claiming status as political prisoners. Dora Lewis (right), a Woman's Party leader, could barely walk after she was released from jail following a hunger strike in August 1918.

The Suffragist, October 27, 1917

Inez Milholland:
"A question still unanswered"

BEULAH AMIDON

A YEAR AGO on November 25 Inez Milholland laid down her gallant young life "for liberty." The last words she spoke in public at the Los Angeles meeting in the closing days of the 1916 campaign have been repeated to hundreds of thousands of Americans by the golden picket banners at the gates of the White House: "Mr. President, how long must women wait for liberty?"

The question is still unanswered. Because they persisted in asking it, thirty-four American women are in jail today. Worn, emaciated, and suffering, the same vision lights the eyes of these "prisoners of freedom" that used to gleam before Inez Milholland as she lay in her hospital room looking out at the sunshine and the roses, and the far misty mountains.

"It is such a big, clean world," she said to me once. "I lie here and try to remember that somewhere people are petty and cruel and unthinking. I lie here and try to remember that there are people without vision and without any dream of liberty. And I can't believe it." Inez Milholland's sudden, flashing smile lighted her white face. "And I think of the fights, too — the fights all over the world, hot, splendid ones — fights for our visions and our hopes and our faiths. In addition, they are always such simple things we fight for. If they were complex, you could understand the necessity for the struggles we make. But suffrage, you know — it's so easy, and that one man could give it to us. And here four generations of women have beaten the wings of their energy and their strength against that one little barrier — I lie here and try to believe it isn't just some sick fancy of mine."

Another day, weeks later, I saw her again, through the half-opened door. Her black hair lay on the pillow about her face. Her eyes were closed. I thought she was asleep, and I stood looking at her, a spent crusader. But she wasn't asleep, and after a while she opened her eyes and looked at me and smiled.

"You came to say good-bye," she said. "All kinds of good luck in the Middle West. It won't be very long before people will understand. It's not going to be so hard now. Women have shown their power. Good-bye." There were unfamiliar little hesitations between the words, and there wasn't much of the old ring in her voice. Three days later Inez Milholland died.

"It's not going to be so hard now," she said. She could not have foreseen the days ahead. No one could have foreseen them or believed them. Riots, arrests, workhouse sentences, solitary cells, hunger strikes, forcible feeding — who would have believed these things could happen in free America? They are happening today, and women are enduring them, with the same indomitable spirit that carried Inez Milholland westward and still westward, with her plea for freedom, even though she was sick to death. And women will go on enduring them, as long as it is necessary, that the question which she died in the asking may never be silenced until it is answered — "Mr. President, how long must women wait for liberty?"

They are crying salt tears
Over the beautiful beloved body
Of Inez Milholland,
Because they are glad she lived,
Because she loved open-armed,
Throwing love for a cheap thing
Belonging to everybody—
Cheap as sunlight,
And morning air.

Carl Sandburg
from *Cornhuskers*

The 19th Amendment to the U.S. Constitution was approved by the Secretary of State on August 26, 1920, after it was ratified by the necessary 36 states. With some exceptions, women nationally could vote equally with men for the first time in the November 1920 presidential election. August 26 is now celebrated annually as Women's Equality Day.

A police matron, center, arrests suffrage pickets Catherine Flanagan and Madeline Watson outside the White House on August 17, 1917 as a crowd looks on. The women were sentenced to thirty days in the Occoquan Workhouse for "obstructing traffic."

ADDITIONAL RESOURCES

The best place to learn more about Inez is Linda J. Lumsden's biography, *Inez: The Life and Times of Inez Milholland.* (Bloomington, IN: Indiana University Press, 2004).

A radio interview with Professor Lumsden also provides insights on Inez: www.albany.edu/talkinghistory/ualbany/ua-lumsden-inez-milholland-1.mp3 (and also -2.mp3).

The Suffragist is available on microfilm at certain research libraries; printed copies are preserved at the Sewall-Belmont House and Museum in Washington D.C., the former headquarters of the National Woman's Party. Inez's personal papers are in the Schlesinger Library at Harvard University.

Inez is mentioned in the following books on the National Woman's Party and its leaders. Check these and the other titles listed for more extensive bibliographies.

National Woman's Party and Leaders

Bausum, Ann. *With Courage and Cloth: Winning the Fight for a Woman's Right to Vote.* Washington D.C.: National Geographic Society, 2004.

Blatch, Harriot Stanton, and Lutz, Alma. *Challenging Years: The Memoirs of Harriot Stanton Blatch.* New York: G.P. Putnam's Sons, 1940.

DuBois, Ellen Carol. *Harriot Stanton Blatch and the Winning of Woman Suffrage.* New Haven, CT: Yale University Press, 1997.

Ford, Linda. *Iron-Jawed Angels: The Suffrage Militancy of the National Woman's Party, 1912–1920.* Lanham, Md.: University Press of America, 1991.

Irwin, Inez Haynes. *The Story of Alice Paul.* New York: Harcourt, Brace and Co., 1921.

Lunardini, Christine. *From Equal Suffrage to Equal Rights: Alice Paul and the National Woman's Party, 1910–1928.* New York: New York University Press, 1986.

Stevens, Doris. *Jailed for Freedom.* New York: Boni and Liveright, 1920.

Walton, Mary. *A Woman's Crusade: Alice Paul and the Battle for the Ballot.* New York: Palgrave MacMillan, 2010.

Zahniser, J.D., and Fry, Amelia. *Alice Paul: Claiming Power.* New York: Oxford, 2014.

Selected Books on the Woman Suffrage Movement

Anthony, Susan B., et al, eds. *History of Woman Suffrage.* Rochester, NY: S.B. Anthony, 1889.

Catt, Carrie Chapman & Shuler, Nettie Rogers. *Woman Suffrage and Politics, The Inner Story of the Suffrage Movement.* New York: C. Scribner's Sons, 1923.

Cooney, Robert P. J., Jr. *Winning the Vote: The Triumph of the American Woman Suffrage Movement.* Santa Cruz, CA: American Graphic Press, 2005.

Flexner, Eleanor. *Century of Struggle, The Woman's Rights Movement in the United States.* Cambridge: Belknap Press of Harvard University Press, 1959.

Florey, Kenneth. *Women's Suffrage Memorabilia: An Illustrated Historical Study.* Jefferson, N.C.: McFarland and Co., 2013.

Graham, Sara. *Woman Suffrage and the New Democracy.* New Haven, CT: Yale University Press, 1996.

Hine, Darlene, et al, eds. *Black Women in America, An Historical Encyclopedia.* Bloomington, IN: Indiana University Press, 1993.

James, Edward, et al, eds. *Notable American Women, A Biographical Dictionary.* Cambridge: Belknap Press of Harvard University Press, 1991.

Terborg-Penn, Rosalyn. *African American Women in the Struggle for the Vote, 1850–1920.* Bloomington, IN: Indiana University Press, 1998.

Ward, Geoffrey C. *Not For Ourselves Alone: The Story of Elizabeth Cady Stanton & Susan B. Anthony.* New York: Alfred A. Knopf, 1999.

Wheeler, Marjorie Spruill, ed. *One Woman, One Vote.* Troutland, OR: New Sage Press, 1995.

Videos

California Women Win the Vote, Martha Wheelock, Wild West Women, 2011
Iron Jawed Angels, Katja Von Garnier, HBO Studios, 2004
Not for Ourselves Alone, Ken Burns, PBS, 2004
One Woman, One Vote, Ruth Pollak, PBS, 1995

Historic Centers and Websites

There are a growing number of online resources on the woman suffrage movement. More information, including manuscript and photographic archives, source material, historic displays, biographies, lesson plans, and online exhibits can be found at the following institutions and websites:

Library of Congress – loc.gov
National Archives – archives.gov
National Women's History Museum – nwhm.org
National Women's History Project – nwhp.org
Newseum – newseum.org
Paulsdale – alicepaul.org
Schlesinger Library – radcliffe.harvard.edu/schlesinger-library; oasis.lib.harvard.edu/oasis/deliver/~sch00193 [Inez's papers]
Sewall-Belmont House and Museum – sewallbelmont.org
Susan B. Anthony Center for Women's Leadership – rochester.edu/ sba/suffragehistory
Susan B. Anthony House and Museum – susanbanthonyhouse.org
Turning Point Suffragist Memorial – suffragistmemorial.org
Vassar College – vassar.edu; vcencyclopedia.vassar.edu/alumni/ inez-milholland.html
Women's Rights National Historical Park – nps.gov/wori

Boissevain News USA [Family Site] – boissevain.us/inezmilholland

A Lesson Plan on Inez is available at: adkhistorycenter.org/edu/pdf/
    WomenOfThePast.pdf
Suffrage History - LetsRocktheCradle.com
Suffrage Centennials – suffragecentennials.com
Suffrage Wagon News Channel – suffragewagon.org
womenshistory.about.com
American History TV (series.c-span.org/History/):
    American Artifacts: Women's Suffrage Parade Centennial
    American Artifacts: Alice Paul & the Women's Suffrage
    Movement

Robert P. J. Cooney, Jr. is the author and designer of "Winning the Vote: The Triumph of the American Woman Suffrage Movement," which documents women's long struggle for political equality. This landmark book explains the long and diverse movement and includes nearly one thousand rare historic photographs and illustrations uncovered during his twelve years of research. Mr. Cooney started the Woman Suffrage Media Project in 1993 to help popularize this nonviolent, grassroots movement, and has consulted on numerous publications, films, and special projects. An editor and graphic designer, he also designed and co-edited "The Power of the People: Active Nonviolence in the United States," an illustrated review of the evolution of nonviolent movements over two and a half centuries, including the drive for equal suffrage.

The **Sewall-Belmont House and Museum** in Washington D.C. preserves the archives from the National Woman's Party's campaigns for both the 19th Amendment and the Equal Rights Amendment. Documents and photographs from the suffrage movement, including those relating to participants like Inez, are kept here and in the Library of Congress. Visit sewallbelmont.org and loc.gov.

The **National Women's History Project** in Santa Rosa, California, coordinates the annual National Women's History Month celebrations every March, honors Equality Day in August, and provides information on multicultural American women throughout the year. The Project's mission is to "Write Women Back into History." Visit nwhp.org.

Also by Robert P. J. Cooney, Jr.

WINNING THE VOTE

THE TRIUMPH OF THE
AMERICAN WOMAN SUFFRAGE MOVEMENT

Named one of the "Five Best Books" on the subject by The Wall Street Journal, this award-winning history covers three generations of suffragists over 72 years, detailing their victories and defeats and profiling over 75 leaders and activists, including Inez Milholland. The elegant, oversize hardback contains hundreds of historic photographs, color illustrations, and original leaflets, buttons, and posters that bring the movement to life. "Winning the Vote" captures the excitement and passion of this early civil rights movement and tells the compelling story of how suffragists finally achieved their historic victory for all women in 1920.

496 pages   9" x 12"   Clothbound, dust jacket   Bibliography   Index

ISBN 0-9770095-0-5 $85.00

Special Collector's Edition in Slipcase $250.00

Order from NWHP.org

Visit AmericanGraphicPress.com